SNIPPETS

Charlotte Zolotow

SNIPPETS

A Gathering of
Poems, Pictures, and Possibilities...

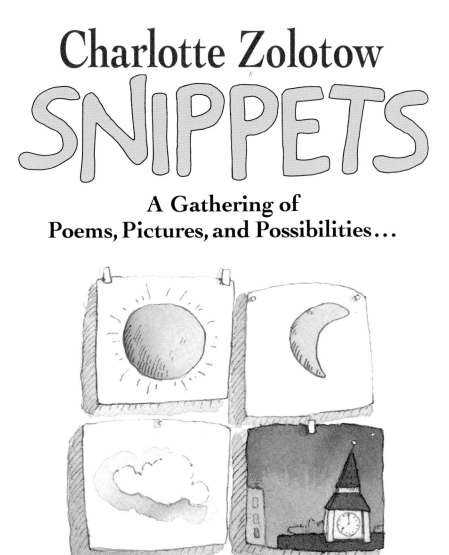

Illustrations by Melissa Sweet

HarperCollinsPublishers

"Snapshot" is adapted by the author from *This Quiet Lady* by Charlotte Zolotow. Text © 1992 by Charlotte Zolotow. By permission of Greenwillow Books, a division of William Morrow & Company, Inc.

"Sunday Morning Walk" and "The Daffodils" are adapted by the author from *One Step, Two...* by Charlotte Zolotow. Text © 1955, 1981 by Charlotte Zolotow. By permission of Greenwillow Books, a division of William Morrow & Company, Inc.

"The Pond," "Milkweed," and "The Kitten" are adapted by the author from *Say It!* by Charlotte Zolotow. Text © 1980 by Charlotte Zolotow. By permission of Greenwillow Books, a division of William Morrow & Company, Inc.

Snippets not credited above appear in books published by HarperCollins Publishers.

Library of Congress Cataloging-in-Publication Data
Zolotow, Charlotte, date
    Snippets : a gathering of poems, pictures, and possibilities... /
by Charlotte Zolotow ; illustrations by Melissa Sweet.
        p.   cm.
    Summary: A collection of verses selected from earlier books by
Charlotte Zolotow.
    ISBN 0-06-020818-X. — ISBN 0-06-020819-8 (lib. bdg.)
    1. Children's poetry, American.   [1. American poetry.]
I. Sweet, Melissa, ill.   II. Title.
PS3549.O63A6   1993   91-37751
811'.54—dc20   CIP
                                                                  AC

To Aileen Fisher, with love
—Charlotte

To Jenny
—Melissa

MORNING

wake up wake up wake up
the trees are winging
the birds are singing
things are thinging
    WAKE UP!

A SQUIRREL

A squirrel
races halfway down a tree trunk
and stops,
spraddled,
as though he had grown out of it.
Then he leaps to the grass,
hops, pauses, hops,
until he has crossed the sidewalk.
He stops in front
of a little girl on a bench
and stands up
on his hind legs,
holding his paws
against his heart,
swishing his tail nervously
waiting for nuts.

THE DRINKING FOUNTAIN

A little girl and a little boy
on a hot day in the park
leaned over the water fountain together.
They could feel each other's hair against their cheeks
as the water bubbled up
cold and sweet
straight into their faces,
wetting their skin,
running down their necks.
The iciness of it
made them laugh.

THE PRESENT

Last Christmas
I half didn't want
to give you your present,
I wanted it so much for myself.

You told me later
you half didn't want to give me mine,
you wanted it so much yourself.

But when we each unwrapped our present
it was the *same* book
and we read out loud

together!

POSSIBILITIES

I'll climb the highest mountain
and bring you
a stone
from the top.

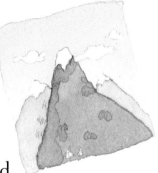

I'll pick the pinkest rose in the world
and bring it home for you.

I'll break rocks in half for you
and swim across oceans
to bring you coral
from the bottom of the sea.

If you want
I'll do arithmetic for you.

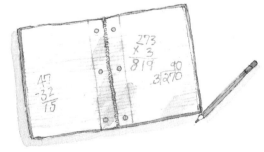

WINTER

We walk together
through the snow.
It's on your hat,
it's in your hair,
it's on your scarf.
Your cheeks are red.
But it's cold
white and bright and cold.

Oh hold my hand!

VALENTINE'S DAY

One day
a little girl woke up
and the breakfast table
had envelopes for her.
"For me?" she asked.
"For you," her mother said.
The little girl opened them.
There were red hearts with white lace,
and lace squares with purple violets.
There were roses with stems
and little poems
that said
"I LOVE YOU!"

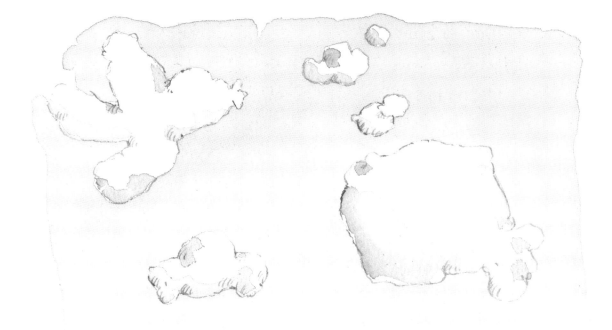

CLOUDS

Do you know what I'll do
on my walk?

I'll look at the clouds
and tell you the shapes
when I get home.

BEST FRIENDS

I know everything about John
and he knows everything about me.
He can't spell!
But I can't multiply,
so we help each other.
But John's the only one
who knows I sleep with the light on at night,
and I'm the only one who knows
he's afraid of cats.
John is my best friend, and I'm his!

FRIENDS

We can sit on the steps
in the sun
and not say anything.
It's nice.
But when I go home,
I sometimes can't wait for dinner to end
so I can call you.
But sometimes you call me first.

AT NIGHT

Do you know what I'll do
in the night?

If you have a nightmare
I'll come
and blow it away.

IN BED

When I am in bed
I hear
footsteps of the night
sharp
like the crackling of a dead leaf
in the stillness.
Then my mother laughs
downstairs.

SNAPSHOT

This young woman
with long hair
blowing in the wind
was my mother
long ago
before I was born.

A FATHER

I'd like a father
who would understand why
I don't want to wear
that green shirt.
He'd say to my mother,
"You never were a boy.
You don't know."

NO RULES

When I have a little girl
there will be no rules.
Nobody will tell her in winter
to stop eating snow
or in summer
to come out of the ocean
even if she's turning blue.
A bath once a week will be enough.
And her mother will never say,
"When you grow up, you'll understand the rules."

BROTHERS

If it weren't for you
I'd be the only child
and I could watch any program I wanted on TV
and keep the light on late at night
to read in bed.
No one would know
if it weren't for you.
   I could have a room of my own,
and I could cry without anyone knowing
and the dog would be just mine.
   But it is true
I'd be alone with the grown-ups

if it weren't for you!

LITTLE GIRL'S DREAM

Someday I'm going to walk
through this same house
and find a room
I've never seen before,
and in it
there will be
shelf after shelf
filled
with dolls.

MY GRANDFATHER

I can still feel
him carrying me.
His arms were strong
and he smelled of powder
and tobacco.
Sometimes he let me
warm my hands
around his pipe.

SUNDAY MORNING WALK

Suddenly the bells of the church
burst into music
like a flock of birds in the sky.
The little girl took her mother's hand
and stood still, listening
until the bells stopped
and everything
was still.

EASTER

One morning
the air was soft and warm
and the birds were singing outside.
A little girl went downstairs,
and there was a basket with shiny green grass
and a chocolate egg
with white icing.
"Happy Easter," her mother said.

THE WISH

"Mr. Rabbit, will you help me?" the little girl said.

"I want to give my mother something she likes
for her birthday."

"Something she likes is a good present," said Mr. Rabbit.

"She likes blue," the little girl said.

"Lakes are blue," said the rabbit.

"But I can't give her a lake, you know," said the little girl.

"Stars are blue."

"I can't give stars," the little girl said,

"but I would

if I could.

The sky and the stars and the lake.

I'd give all of them to her!"

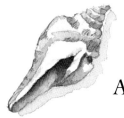

A PROMISE

The little girl kissed her mother good-by.
"Do you know what I'll do
at the seashore?" she asked.

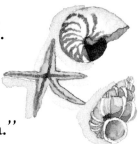

"I'll bring you a shell
to hold the sound of the sea."

THE SHELL

At the beach
a little boy
picks up a shell.
It is twisted
pink and grey
and sandy inside.
He wonders
who lived in it
before it was washed up
from the sea.

LIGHTNING

It shoots through the sky
like a streak of starlight
a flash—beautiful and fast.

A little brown sandpiper
skids across the sand
so swiftly
he is gone
before the light leaves the sky.

PIGEONS

A gray-blue pigeon
blows up his feathers
and struts
across the path
to other pigeons
waiting in the grass.
An old man
scatters bread crumbs
and the pigeons
ripple up to his feet
in a blue and silver wave.

THE CITY

In the storm-darkened city
a little boy
closes his book
and gets up
to look out the window.
Below him on the street
the lighted store windows
shine on the wet sidewalks
and every flash of lightning
shows people running by,
newspapers over their heads
or umbrellas held down in front of them
to buffet the wind and the rain.
The automobile tires
make a swish-swishing sound
as they pass.

A DOG

A little boy
is alone
in his room.
Outside
someone is raking leaves
and a bare tree branch
brushes his window.

Suddenly a wet cold nose
nuzzles his hand
and a furry head
pushes it
for a pat.

THE DAFFODILS

A little girl
bent down to smell
the daffodils
and her nose was tipped
with yellow pollen powder.
She stopped to pet
her own big dog
and he licked off the yellow
with his kiss.

THE POND

A little girl
stood
and saw herself
upside down
in the smooth water of the pond.

Then the wind rose
and suddenly
she became
a million zigzags
the color of her dress.

WIND

Do you know what I'll do when the wind blows?

I'll put it in a bottle
and let it loose
in summer
when the house is hot.

HOT CITY NIGHT

Oh it was a hot night!
The heat was like a feathered bird
over the city.
The bird folded its wings,
and the pink and orange plumage
of sunset
was covered
by the fleecy gray and purple sky.

THE CAT

There is a cat
prowling through the garden
like a small tiger
looking for her prey.
But with a lovely flacking sound
all the birds
       fly away.

THE BASEBALL GAME

First there is the thunk of the bat,
then the curve of the ball
in the air,
and then
the thick smack
as it lands in the catcher's glove.

MILKWEED

In the soft summer air
a piece of fluff from some milkweed
drifts by
like a little floating cloud
full of seeds.

THE MOON

The moon,
reflected in the pond,
seemed so close
the little girl felt
she could reach into the smooth black water
and hold the moon in her hands.

AUTUMN

What I love best
in the fall
are chrysanthemums.
I love the trees red and gold and brown
and the wild wind blowing
and the squirrels gathering nuts.
But what I love best
are the chrysanthemums
tangled and shaggy
and smelling like spice.

THE KITTEN

A small black kitten
scampers down a driveway
and stands paw deep
in a pool of orange and brown leaves.

He curves his paw
and scrambles away—
scurry, scramble, scurry
the leaves
swirl around him.

HALLOWEEN

The little girl stood by the door
and every time the bell rang
she asked
the ghosts and witches and tigers and tramps who came,
"What's your name?"
But all they would say was
                    "TRICK OR TREAT?"
But one little witch said,
"Happy Halloween,"
as he went off
into the night.

RIVER IN WINTER

The ice moves slowly
                        down the river.
The gulls
            are circling high
Grey and white
grey and white
against
            the
                    grey-blue
                            sky!

WHAT WAS IT LIKE

"What was it like
when you were as old as I am now?"
a little girl asked her mother.
"Well, when I went to bed,"
her mother said,
"the room was dark
the clocks ticked
grown-ups talked downstairs
the stars shone in the sky
and I could hear the wind in the trees outside
before I hugged my mother good night
the way you do now."

BEGINNINGS

The end of winter
when the snow melts
and the birds come back
is the beginning of spring.
The end of anything is
the beginning
of something else.

Charlotte Zolotow's "snippets" appear in the following books: